KEEPING CREATION

KEEPING CREATION

A 5-WEEK STUDY

CALEB CRAY HAYNES | RYAN FASANI | MEGAN M. PARDUE | TODD WOMACK

f▸

THE FOUNDRY
PUBLISHING®

Cover design: Caines Design
Interior design: Sharon Page

The internet addresses, email addresses, and phone numbers in this book are accurate at the time of publication. They are provided as a resource. The Foundry Publishing does not endorse them or vouch for their content or permanence.

CONTENTS

FOREWORD   6
A People of Creation
Nell Becker Sweeden

UNIT ONE   12
Introduction: A Human Thing
Caleb Cray Haynes

UNIT TWO   30
Creationivity (Genesis 1)
Caleb Cray Haynes

UNIT THREE   50
Our First Vocation (Genesis 2)
Ryan Fasani

UNIT FOUR   68
Rediscovering God's Limits (Genesis 3)
Megan M. Pardue

UNIT FIVE   88
I Am We (Genesis 4)
Todd Womack

ABOUT THE AUTHORS   108

FOREWORD
A PEOPLE OF CREATION

The L<small>ORD</small> spoke to Moses, saying: "Speak to all the
congregation of the Israelites and say to them:
You shall be holy, for I the L<small>ORD</small> your God am holy."
—Leviticus 19:1–2 (NRSVUE)

When Jesus saw the crowds, he went up the
mountain, and after he sat down, his disciples came to
him. And he began to speak and taught them,
saying: "Blessed are the poor in spirit,
for theirs is the kingdom of heaven."
—Matthew 5:1–3 (NRSVUE)

YAHWEH CALLS the people Israel into relationship in order to reveal the way of God's reign. The way of God, revealed in relationship, is meant to touch every aspect of life. Similarly, Jesus invited his followers into *the way*, incarnated in his own life and ministry. Faithfulness for God's people meant embracing an entire lifestyle that united a community. Faithfulness was deeply interwoven with all the elements of daily livelihood—care for the land, for the animals, for the household members, and welcoming strangers. The people's faith and trust in God went hand in hand with decisions of economic daily life and with the political makeup and social fabric of the broader community. In contrast, contemporary Western Christian understandings of following Jesus often center on the decision of the heart. As modern influences and constructs have deeply shaped Christian faith and expression, there is a tendency to compartmentalize faith expression and worship of God separately from daily work and life in the broader world.

A few years ago, I had the privilege of working alongside intercultural studies professor Randy Woodley in Portland, Oregon. Drawing on his Native American heritage, way of life, and theological frame of reference, Randy often reminded those of us who were white theology professors—such as myself and my husband—that to be Native American means something so much more than bloodline. It doesn't matter what percentage of a tribe one carries because to be Native American is to embrace a certain way of life and harmony with the earth and fellow humans. If one isn't living in an indigenous way in harmony with people, animals, and the land, bloodline has little meaning. Rather, one's identity and belonging to a people are evidenced by what one does and how one acts in relationship with others and the world around them.

Today across our globe, many indigenous peoples have been displaced or have become minority populations in their territories, yet the way of life they embody has a clear similarity to the social-cultural makeup of a Hebrew way of life. Both center around relational interconnectedness with the natural world and a respect for and dependency on the mysterious and sovereign acts of the Creator. Both concern themselves with the delicate balance and relationship humans have with the land and animals upon which we depend for survival; therefore, they hold alternative understandings of time and resources as compared to a more results-based, modern world.

In this book, the authors introduce a word that is prevalent in multiple countries of the southern portion of Africa, *ubuntu*, which can be translated, "I am because we are." More than a concept or saying, *ubuntu* reflects a way of life. *Ubuntu* is about identity, belonging, and source of being. "I am because we are" infiltrates all of life and action. I have had the privilege of encountering many Christian brothers and sisters throughout the vast continent of Africa who embody this beautiful reflection of interdependence and care, together with an unwavering trust in God as the source of being. Similarly, it returns us to the way of Jesus and God's people reflected in Scripture.

In contrast, my own upbringing in the United States centered more on my personal development as an individual who was part of a nuclear family unit and also my broader Christian family, which is a reflection of the time and place I was born in history. Yet the body of Christ around the world has opened my eyes to new understanding. "I am because we are" invites me to embrace faithfulness to God by seeking to live in harmony with God's intention for humanity, as well as recognizing how I must change and adapt out of concern for the well-being of my neighbor. *Ubuntu* reflects an expansive picture of how the body of Christ is called to live into God's reign with each act of our lives, daily behaviors, trust, and affections.

In *Keeping Creation*, the authors narrate a refreshing return to God's call on humanity to care for and tend the earth for the flourishing of *all* creation. Reading Genesis 1–4 through the lens of contemporary challenges, each unit of study invites the reader toward a renewed

Christian way of life in the world. This way of life returns us to God's original call that interconnected us with responsibility with and for our Lord's creation. The authors reveal how returning to this call and allowing it to infiltrate our lives anew can mitigate both environmental degradation and neglect *and* our cultural neglect of caring for fellow human beings. Returning to God's creation of humanity out of dust—earth and soil—and the Spirit, the authors remind readers of humanity's total dependence on God and the natural finitude and limitations of what it means to be human. To be humans created in God's image directs us to trust in God's ways above human ways, which also cultivates grace and patience with ourselves and one another in living and learning. Returning to creation does not require that we add more things to our day or work more efficiently but simply to embrace the intentional, albeit slow and steady, work of caring for the land and living in harmony with God's creation, as God intended it.

The authors' reflections in the following pages invite us into a journey together. May the Lord open our eyes and ears. May the Lord change our hearts and lives. May we be united in our unwavering trust in God to seek faithfulness to and be transformed by our original call as humans.

Nell Becker Sweeden

UNIT ONE
INTRODUCTION
A HUMAN THING
CALEB CRAY HAYNES

ON A COOL MARCH MORNING I put on a tie and went downtown to a House Commerce Committee hearing for a bill in the Tennessee State Legislature. I was there with a group of others looking to take a stand for caring for neighbor and earth. We gathered in opposition to a bill that would essentially strip the local rights of governments to have any say in fossil fuel and other new energy infrastructure (like pipelines, storage tanks, and the like) coming through their communities and neighborhoods. The potential ramifications of this bill's passage could be immense, especially if other states decided to follow suit. If passed, this bill would severely limit the ability of local elected officials to oppose such development, even when it affects the health and safety of the people and the land of their communities. Essentially, it meant substantial opportunities for big energy conglomerates to come and do as they please, where they please, usually justified by the notion that "it's good for the economy." Unfortunately, the economy is usually driven by overconsumption, and this kind of consumerism literally consumes the earth, the landscape, and the health of all its inhabitants. It sounds like a no-brainer, right? It's better when locals do *not* have their voice taken away in the name of energy development.

Ten different people testified—environmental lawyers, activists, pastors, experts, and ordinary citizens. Each eloquently and compellingly shared what a *bad idea* this bill was. But what I witnessed that morning, unfortunately, was something we hear enough about but maybe don't often get to see so clearly, namely: polarization, tribalism, and indifference toward those not on "your" side.

My jaw hung open as I watched the proceedings. Some politicians seemed to care and be interested in the testimonies of opposition but didn't conclude it to be worth the risk of departing from the party line. I realized that day there was only one reason someone could hear all the presented facts, stories, and speeches yet still come away unmoved: *because that's the other team, and we can't vote with "them," can we?*

There seemed to be numerous reasons to stand together on these critical issues and few reasons to stand apart. On something that is meant to be unifying—like taking care of the people and planet around us—it seemed that many people's only concern that day was knowing which kingdom they were part of. The bill passed.

There is no denying that the issues of life and politics have many angles, sides, and facets to be considered. But what happens when the very lens through which we see the world becomes so colored by our selected group that we end up actually missing the good thing God is calling us to see? I'm left wondering—as a Christian who is called, alongside all other Christians, to care for creation—how this has gotten so complicated. What group determines our concerns and commitments? Whose kingdom are we *actually* part of?

IN THE TEXT

*Now after John was arrested, Jesus came to Galilee
proclaiming the good news of God and saying, "The
time is fulfilled, and the kingdom of God has come near;
repent, and believe in the good news."*
—Mark 1:14–15 (NRSVUE)

Sometimes Christians get so caught up in the worldly culture of king
and country that we forget the heavenly kingdom we are part of has its
own culture and its own agenda—namely, the salvation of the world.
Jesus speaks about the kingdom of God like a broken record, referring
to it more than a hundred times in the Gospels. For first-century folks,
"kingdom" is a loaded term. Kingdom, as Jesus's listeners would have
understood it, is full of political and economic meaning. Jesus referenc-
ing God's here-yet-still-arriving reign on earth is his way of telling us
that our heavenly citizenship is also very earthy. We find in Jesus our
invitation and call to participate in this coming kingdom of God now,
here, with our feet on the ground!

Our relationship with God has to do with how we share our resources, break our bread together, forgive each other, show compassion, and
offer hospitality. It is about everything that makes life as God intended it to be. Thus, to talk about politics and economics is to talk about
every area of life that matters. It is about how we do life together in
the world, and Jesus certainly had a lot to say about that! Jesus is con-

tinually inviting us into a way of seeing the world that isn't *this side* or *that side* but a *way* marked by love and by the beauty of the kingdom of heaven.

The first principle of the kingdom of God is that it includes everything.
—Wendell Berry[1]

*The L*ORD *spoke to Moses, saying: "Speak to all the*
congregation of the Israelites and say to them:
*You shall be holy, for I the L*ORD *your God am holy."*
—*Leviticus 19:1–2 (NRSVUE)*

The book of Leviticus is a wonderful text that helps us further understand how living within God's politics and economy has to do with all things! Particularly, as we get into chapter 19 and what we refer to as the "holiness code," we find it is incredibly rich with meaning for us. It starts with God saying, "Be holy, for I the Lord your God am holy," and follows with how we breed animals, sow seeds, eat crops, present and use our bodies, consume sacrifices, pay employees, and welcome refugees! These verses aren't arbitrary rules to follow. Leviticus isn't here to

1. Wendell Berry, "Two Economies," *Review & Expositor* Vol. 81, No. 2 (May 1984), 209. http://worldwisdom.com/public/viewpdf/default.aspx?article-title=Two_Economies_by_Wendell_Berry.pdf.

torture us as we attempt to muster up enough energy to jump through God's hoops. These words are about issues of love, justice, and what it means to be holy because God is holy.

Essentially, we learn that holy living has something to say about everything because, in the end, there are no areas of creation that God doesn't care about! After all, all of creation is the Lord's (Psalm 24:1). Further, God finds joy when creation is unfolding the way it was created to. All of it matters because everything is included within God's redemptive work in the world and ultimately through Christ, through whom "God was pleased to reconcile to himself all things, whether things on earth or in heaven, by making peace through the blood of his cross (Colossians 1:20, NRSVUE).

Today, in an age where we've commodified almost everything, we often attempt to compartmentalize the world in our minds. Our consumer mind wants to see the world like a vending machine, where we put in our money, click the right number, and get the corresponding packaged good. Seeing the world this way views one part of creation as untethered from all the other parts. Yet all one has to do is choose any item and begin peeling back the layers. Something as simple as bread, for instance, holds multiple ingredients, each dependent on healthy soil, which is dependent upon proper light, water, and microbiology. Further, each crop is tethered to the life of the farmer and the famer's well-being.

When we zoom in further to see the infinitesimal layers or zoom out to see how we all exist on the same sphere floating in space, we learn that all life is woven together. We find that our holy Creator God has made a world that is interconnected more than we can imagine! What occurs on one side of the planet affects the other side of the planet. How I treat the land has a direct effect on my neighbors. The more we learn—from healthy ecosystems in the jungle to the healthy biome inside our gut—the more we find that a healthy creation is dependent on all the pieces and parts working together in beautiful tandem. Therefore, caring for creation is a matter of the interconnectedness of all life. How well we care for or neglect creation directly affects how well we love our neighbor, human and nonhuman alike.

When God began to create the
heavens and the earth . . .
—Genesis 1:1 (NRSVUE)

As it happens, creation care is not an isolated cause set apart from the rest of life. In order to talk about caring for creation, we have to talk about *all of creation*—politics, economics, food, energy, freedom, and our faith. Creation involves everything we see, every noise we hear, every morsel we taste, every item we touch, every person we've ever met or heard of, and every choice we've ever made! It's deep, it's wide, it's all-encompassing, and it's holistic in nature because, at its core, that's what nature is—an interconnected whole teeming with life.

Caring for this earth, although it involves political thinking and action, is not partisan. Think about it! Caring for our common home that we share with all people everywhere and all forms of life is not something dreamed up by politicians but is instead a joyful command from our Creator. Further, it is part of our divinely given DNA as the people of God, which we will explore more in the units ahead. If we Christians allow cultural politics or labels to influence our sacred role as God's stewards on earth, we will miss out on the essential calling and work our Creator has placed us here for.

In the pages ahead we will share stories and explore what the first four chapters of Genesis can teach us about our relationship with creation. The intent of this book is not merely to be a Bible study on Genesis, but it is to allow these early chapters of our Bible to shape us in a way that creates a deeper awareness of our ancient task of keeping creation. This book does not engage in debate over the age of the planet but approaches Scripture from the perspective that the early chapters in Genesis are mythic in proportion—that is, they do the work of giving us deep truth about our relationship with God, creation, and one another. In that work, we find they are even poetic in nature as they convey to us meaning that transcends data and lifts up intent, purpose, and the creativity of our God.

IN OUR WORLD TODAY

They have devastated her; desolate, she cries out to me
in distress: "The whole land is desolate,
and no one seems to care."
—Jeremiah 12:11 (CEB)

On another lovely spring day, I found myself preparing some new garden beds at a local middle school so students could learn about growing their own food. One of the teachers came meandering out the side door to take a look. I'll always remember the utterly puzzled look on his face as he gazed about. Not even meeting my eyes, he scratched his head and skeptically inquired, "So what is this, some kind of *tree-hugger* thing?"

I was thinking, *You mean engaging with the soil? Learning where our food comes from? Growing a garden? Eating?*

I simply responded, "No, this a human thing."

The earth is undergoing deep suffering. Creation is groaning, waiting for us all to embrace care for this place not as something separate from ourselves or as extra credit, and not because we have a "green thumb" or some extra time on our hands (see Jeremiah 12:10–11; Hosea 4:1–3; Romans 8:22). We must reawaken to the work of caring for creation because, as we learn from our inception, it's a deeply human thing.

At current consumption rates, soon there will be no more glaciers in Glacier National Park.[2] Every single day we are losing around two hundred thousand acres of our global rainforests, often referred to as "the lungs of our planet."[3] There is now so much human-generated greenhouse gas trapped in our atmosphere that we are altering earth's physical attributes with its interconnected and carefully balanced systems.[4] Our oceanic ecosystems are falling apart as coral reefs decay due to warming waters and acidification; meanwhile, fishing stocks are depleting at even faster rates.[5] Honeybee colonies continue to collapse around the world, approaching a catastrophic tipping point in nature.[6] Globally, we lose seventy-five billion metric tons of fertile soil from arable land each year due to overworked topsoil, which is severely threatening the way we grow our food.[7] Today, exposure to contaminated air, wa-

2. "Soon" can mean different things depending on whom you ask, but the longest estimates are no later than the turn of the century (the year 2100). "Status of Glaciers in Glacier National Park," Northern Rocky Mountain Science Center (April 2016), https://www.usgs.gov/centers/norock/science/status-glaciers-glacier-national-park. Other experts say it could be as early as 2030. "Overview of Glacier National Park's Glaciers," National Park Service (August 2022), https://www.nps.gov/glac/learn/nature/glaciersoverview.htm.

3. "About the Rainforest: Rainforest Facts" (Rain-Tree Publishers, 2019), https://www.rain-tree.com/facts.htm.

4. "Sixth Assessment Report" (The Intergovernmental Panel on Climate Change [IPCC], 2021–2022), https://www.ipcc.ch/assessment-report/ar6/.

5. "Ocean Acidification" (Smithsonian Ocean, April 2018), https://ocean.si.edu/ocean-life/invertebrates/ocean-acidification.

6. "Colony Collapse Disorder" (United States Environmental Protection Agency, 2021), https://www.epa.gov/pollinator-protection/colony-collapse-disorder.

7. "Soil Fertility and Erosion" (Global Agriculture, n.d.), https://www.globalagriculture.org/report-topics/soil-fertility-and-erosion/soil-fertility-and-erosion.html.

ter, or soil takes three times as many lives around the world as AIDS, tuberculosis, and malaria combined.[8]

These facts are markers of fundamental brokenness within creation. These circumstances are beyond tragic—they are horrific. When the fabric of creation experiences deterioration, humanity suffers. If the planet does not thrive, we do not thrive. We are not people *on* a planet but people *of* a planet. Being *citizens of earth* is not in opposition to being citizens of the kingdom of God. Rather, it is the embodiment of our calling to care for this place and to be God's means of proclaiming good news to the entire world!

In view of this breakdown in creation and our calling to care, how might the people of God respond? Ignoring these issues only harms more people we are called to love. Caring for creation is a God-given task for us all. As Christians who are called to love like God loves, how can we look at the brokenness of creation, and all those in harm's way, and not be moved?

Humanity is beautifully intertwined with creation, not for the ultimate consumption of the world but for the flourishing of God's handiwork. When all parts of the ecosystem are functioning in harmony, it's as if all of nature is joined together in a choir, praising God. This flourishing

8. Philip J. Landrigan, Richard Fuller, Nereus J R Acosta, Olusoji Adeyi, Robert Arnold, Niladri Basu, et al., "The *Lancet* Commission on Pollution and Health, *Lancet*, vol. 391, iss. 10119: October 2017, 462–512.

of creation glorifies God. This is one reason that some of the psalms depict all creatures together singing. Read Psalm 148.

PSALM 148 (NRSVUE)

Praise the LORD!
Praise the LORD from the heavens;
praise him in the heights!
Praise him, all his angels;
praise him, all his host!

Praise him, sun and moon;
praise him, all you shining stars!
Praise him, you highest heavens,
and you waters above the heavens!

Let them praise the name of the LORD,
for he commanded and they were created.
He established them forever and ever;
he fixed their bounds, which cannot be passed.

Praise the LORD from the earth,
you sea monsters and all deeps,
fire and hail, snow and frost,
stormy wind fulfilling his command!

Mountains and all hills,
fruit trees and all cedars!
Wild animals and all cattle,
creeping things and flying birds!

Kings of the earth and all peoples,
princes and all rulers of the earth!
Young men and women alike,
old and young together!

Let them praise the name of the LORD,
for his name alone is exalted;
his glory is above earth and heaven.
He has raised up a horn for his people,
praise for all his faithful,
for the people of Israel who are close to him.
Praise the LORD!

REFLECT AND DISCUSS

- What are your thoughts after reading or hearing Psalm 148? What stands out to you?

- How have you experienced the idea of caring for creation being politicized or polarizing?

- How is it helpful for us to look at creation care through the lens of holiness?

- Can you think of some reasons why earth care *is* people care?

- How do you see caring for creation as a Christian value?

- Share about a time when you had an experience in nature that was meaningful.

- What are you questioning? What, if anything, rubs you the wrong way in conversations about creation care? Attempt to spend a few moments identifying why this conversation may be uncomfortable.

- What about the creation care discussion encourages you as a Christian?

- Discuss how humans harming God's creation might make God feel.

- Spend time with your group dialoguing about the intersection of creation care and worshiping the Creator.

RESPOND

Grow Outward

Start three conversations with friends, family members, or neighbors this week about some of the things we have discussed in this first unit. If you know someone who loves being outdoors or caring for creation, talk to them about it. What do they appreciate about spending time outside? What are their favorite outdoor activities? What are the connections they make between their faith and creation? If you talk to someone for whom these ideas or concepts are new, or who perhaps doesn't spend time outdoors, share with them one new insight you have gained and one area where you felt challenged in this first unit.

Grow Inward

As you prepare to go through this study, set aside special time to pray. Ask God to help you clear your mind and open your heart to what God has for you here. Again, there can be so much in the way of receiving the word God is planting. We remember Jesus's parable where the seed fell in a variety of places. Pray for good soil so that you may receive the kind of germination God desires for your life.

Form a Green Habit

Living into creation care often involves lots of little decisions—everything from what goes into the waste bin to what lights get left on to the kind of goods we consume and their packaging. Sometimes we tend to think all these little choices don't matter or make any difference, but they really do add up to large-scale change. With your small group or family, choose a new green habit to begin practicing together. Adopting a new practice is always easier when we do it with others. If you need some ideas, check out nazarenesforcreationcare.com/creation-care-tips.

CREATIONIVITY
(GENESIS 1)

CALEB CRAY HAYNES

THERE'S A WORD that my daughter came home from school saying one day, and I'm certain she didn't learn it from us. She sat on the couch looking a little glum. Then she looked at us and said in a frustrated tone, "I'm *bored*!"

Bored—where did that come from? What does my energetic six-year-old who endlessly colors, crafts, and sings know about being bored? As a parent, I was perplexed to find that my creative daughter, so early, could learn and begin to express such a sentiment. Something about the whole thing seemed to catch me by surprise. It makes me wonder: is boredom a hint at something more profound going on within us?

Boredom gives us a framework to peer into deeper halls of human identity because boredom can feel like the antithesis of creativity. Boredom happens when it seems like nothing is cooking. We understand boredom as what happens when the juices aren't flowing. Boredom happens when we feel in some way trapped by the formlessness and emptiness of a day. Boredom seems to be the emptiness of creation.

That's the reason I stopped in my tracks when my little girl—who has artwork hanging on every empty surface of our home—suddenly looked at me and said the b-word!

"Boredom" is a word always pronounced with an "ugh" tone of voice— because, as we all know, no matter who you are or where you live, boredom is not "how it's supposed to be." So how *is* it supposed to be?

IN THE TEXT

In the beginning when God created the heavens and the earth, the earth was a formless void and darkness covered the face of the deep, while a wind from God swept over the face of the waters.
—Genesis 1:1–2 (NRSVA)

The first time we see the name "God" (in Hebrew, *elohim*) in Scripture, it is next to the verb "created" (*bara*). From the very first moment, we discover that our God is a Creator, and the first chapter of our Bible is a story of our God doing what God does best: forming, shaping, making, and—I believe we can safely add—loving.

The second verse of Genesis reveals that the earth was a "formless void" (*tohu* and *bohu*). It was essentially empty, without form, barren, unordered, full of raw potential, a blank canvas, uncreated. This formless void is the necessary emptiness, space, or "boredom" that offers a creative opportunity for God. Here we find that the Wind, or Spirit, of God (*ruach elohim*) was already moving amidst this dark, formless, chaotic water-world. Even in this period of voidness, something was at work.

The Spirit's movement was the divine inhale that exhaled the first Word, "Let there be." Since that very first word was spoken, creation has been unfolding. This divine creative energy that began so long ago continues to pulse through all things and through you and through me still today. It is God's creative fingerprint on the universe. Creation is anything but boring! Clouds and eagles, rivers and salmon, mountains, trees, and kangaroos are testaments to the excitement of all creation! God's creation is beautiful and engaging, and there is always more adventure and discovery to be had within it.

Another factor that makes creation so magnificent is its holistic nature. If we skip ahead to Day 7, we find that creation is whole. All is included. All is as it should be. All is "good," as God declares it. All is holy because it reveals the nature of our Creator. But "complete" is not a word we use here. It's not that creation is *missing* something; rather, creation by its very nature is moving, growing, bearing fruit, and multiplying. Therefore, to call it "complete" would be to misinterpret what Genesis 1 informs us is the nature of this creation: that it is actually a creation of ongoing-ness. Genesis 1 is but a first round of seven days that sparks the beginning of an ever-flowing cycle of seven days. On and on it goes, seven, seven, seven, perfect, whole, "very good," and continuously so.

What God creates in the beginning isn't only creation the noun but also creation the verb. God creates the *work* of creating. Within that which is formless and void, God births creation (see Psalm 90:2, CEB), and from there we find that the beautiful snowball of creative love is now rolling!

Following verses 1 and 2 in Genesis 1, all of the first account of God's creative work unfolds within the next twenty-nine verses. God begins with this pattern of separating and filling. Days 1 through 3, God separates. First, light comes and the separation of light from darkness. Then God creates sky, separating waters above from waters below. By day 3, God is separating the waters below to form dry land and seas. Then Days 4 through 6 are God filling these spaces with sun, moon, stars, fish, birds, cattle, crawly creatures, and eventually humanity.

Let's back up and take a closer look at verse 11. There is a second command on Day 3: "Then God said, 'Let the earth put forth vegetation: plants yielding seed, and fruit trees of every kind on earth that bear fruit with the seed in it.' And it was so" (NRSVUE). The arrival of seeds is the reminder that knit *within* the cosmic order is creation's ability to spring forth more life! There is a rhythm to the original language. The literal Hebrew translation sounds more like, "Let sprouts sprout, seeds seed, and fruit fruit!" This creative empowerment continues in verses 20 and 24, as both water and land are told to produce life.

This capacity for creation to beget more creation is essential for us to grasp. Creation's ability to create is the heartbeat of how God intends for all of matter—including humanity—to exist. This capacity for creation to continue the process of creating—or, rather, the noun-verb "creationivity," as I like to call it—is reinforced even further through the repeated refrain in verses 22 and 28, "be fruitful and multiply." In fact, a literal translation of the text in Genesis 2:3, which ends this entire first creation account, can read, "God rested from all the work he had *created for making.*" Creation's ability to create is at the heartbeat of our beginning story.

Then God said, "Let us make humans in our image,
according to our likeness, and let them have dominion
over the fish of the sea and over the birds of the air and
over the cattle and over all the wild animals
of the earth and over every creeping thing
that creeps upon the earth."

God blessed them, and God said to them, "Be fruitful
and multiply and fill the earth and subdue it and have
dominion over the fish of the sea and over the birds
of the air and over every living thing that
moves upon the earth."
—*Genesis 1:26, 28 (NRSVUE)*

Finally, after literally every other habitat and creature has been created, God creates humans. "Let us make humans in our image," we read at the end of Day 6. We learn that God is "we" in nature. God is relational and a co-creator even within God's self. So we discover that we are also relational beings because we are created in the image of the divine community. Genesis quickly teaches us that we are created for relationship with God, for relationship with creation, and for relationship with one another. Each is connected to the other.

It's hard to miss how late humanity enters the narrative of Genesis 1, isn't it? Why would we be last? If we wrote the story of creation ourselves, I can't help but think we'd arrive by Day 3 at the latest! We find here, early in our story, that we aren't the center of this poetic narrative. We are only *part* of this beautiful creation. Yet, even so, God has left for us arguably the most crucial part to play. I don't think it's any coincidence that humanity was the final piece of these cosmically stunning and creative six days. God does, in fact, have an invaluable role for humanity to fulfill. Just imagine, if you're a good creator and you make an entire world full of wonders, stars, stallions, oceans, whales, coral, fungi, and minerals, the final being you want to create might be an extension of yourself—somebody to be your feet on the ground. This is exactly what God does—we are made in God's very image. We are made to be co-creators with God for the life of the world itself.[1]

Our task is further unpacked when we arrive at some of the most well-known words on the topic of humanity's role in creation: "dominion" and "subdue." Often today we translate these terms to mean we can do whatever we want with creation or that creation is something beneath us, meant to ultimately serve and support us as the superior apex of

---

1. This is the same point Jesus makes in his parables about masters giving stewardship over property to their servants (see Matthew 25:14–30; Luke 12:13–21, 42–48; 16:1–13; 18:18–30; 19:11–27).

creation. But these ideas have no place in the context of Genesis. Dominion is not domination. To subdue is not to oppress. Creation does not exist for our plunder and prosperity; rather, *we* exist as those who are called to the joyful task of stewardship of the natural world, which is the Lord's, not our own.

In order to understand "dominion" and "subdue," we must understand "likeness." As Christians, we know that we come to understand it through our incarnated God, Jesus Christ. There is perhaps no better summation of the kind of dominion and rule that our God embodies than Paul's words in his letter to the Philippians: "Let the same mind be in you that was in Christ Jesus, who, though he existed in the form of God, did not regard equality with God as something to be grasped, but emptied himself, taking the form of a slave, assuming human likeness. And being found in appearance as a human, he humbled himself and became obedient to the point of death—even death on a cross" (2:5–8, NRSVUE). The kind of dominion and rule that mark the reign of God's kingdom, embodied through Jesus Christ, is known by love, humility, gentleness, compassion, and the posture of a servant. God created humanity, in God's own image, to see to it that everything he had already created was well loved. Through our caring hands offered up, fields, trees, beasts, and birds might flourish as they are intended to.

Notice that immediately following "dominion" are listed the three areas that have just been created: the sea, the sky, the land, and all that lives within them. Out of all God's creation, we ourselves are called into fruitfulness and co-creativity but also are charged with stewarding all other forms of life so they might continue to be fruitful as well!

We are not at liberty to use what [God] has lodged in our hands as we please, but as he pleases, who alone is the possessor of heaven and earth, and the Lord of every creature.
—John Wesley[2]

Thus the heavens and the earth were finished and all their multitude. On the sixth day God finished the work that he had done, and he rested on the seventh day from all the work that he had done. So God blessed the seventh day and hallowed it, because on it God rested from all the work that he had done in creation.
—Genesis 2:1–3

Finally, on the seventh day, God rested. No creating. No work. We could even say that this empty day is un-creation. We could even say that this seventh day is formless and void. Sabbath, as it happens, isn't just a good idea; creation itself is contingent upon the practice of sab-

2. John Wesley, "Sermon 51: The Good Steward," http://wesley.nnu.edu/john-wesley/the-sermons-of-john-wesley-1872-edition/sermon-51-the-good-steward.

bath rest. Our rest from work is the necessary empty womb into which new creationivity can be born. It's part of the fabric of the whole thing. So we shouldn't be surprised that our current culture of endless work, limitless growth, unceasing engines, and continual combustion leaves not only ourselves but also the whole of nature broken, drained, depleted, and oppressed.

In the end, freedom came as I realized that boredom wasn't something I needed to solve for my daughter because it was the doorway. Boredom—that moment of un-creation, those times of formlessness and void—are moments we naturally find ourselves having to embrace and journey through in order to finally hear God say again, "Let there be light!"

IN OUR WORLD TODAY

It's more than exciting to be God's stewards, God's hands and feet in creation! Yet, if we aren't cautious, it can become a quick stumble into placing ourselves at the center, rather than remembering that God is the center. Anytime we do this, the end result always turns out for the worse. When our dominion places our motives and desires at the center, it quickly becomes a posture of domination rather than stewardship.

Geologists are now referring to the age we live in as the Anthropocene era. This name for the geological era expresses how humans have altered the surface of our planet and pushed the earth into an age that is dominated by our activity upon it. Since the dawn of time, we've wanted to be the center of all creation. As both Scripture and science prove us wrong, sin always lures us to posture ourselves as our own gods at the center of the created order.[3]

A recent study of the earth's biomass revealed that, out of all mammals alive on Planet Earth today, an astounding 96 percent are humans and our livestock.[4] That means only 4 percent of all mammals alive on earth today are wild animals—in other words, the kinds of animals we see at the zoo like otters, elk, apes, sea lions, bears, dolphins, lemurs, tigers, and so on.

How has this happened? According to a recent article, "On land, in the seas, in the sky, the devastating impact of humans on nature is laid bare in a compelling UN report. One million animal and plant species are now threatened with extinction."[5] Land, seas, and sky—precisely the places for which we are given responsibility ("dominion") at the very beginning.

---

3. John P. Rafferty, "Anthropocene Epoch," *Encyclopedia Britannica*, Septebmer 2022, https://www.britannica.com/science/Anthropocene-Epoch. Although there is disagreement about when the Anthropocene era began, there is consensus that we are no longer in the previous geological epoch of the Holocene and that human involvement and mass colonization of the planet have thrust us into a new era.

4. Yinon M. Bar-On, Rob Phillips, and Ron Milo, "The Biomass Distribution on Earth," PNAS, May 2018 115 (25) 6506–6511, https://www.pnas.org/doi/full/10.1073/pnas.1711842115. (PNAS stands for "Proceedings of the National Academy of Sciences" [of the United States of America]).

5. Matt McGrath, "Nature Crisis: Humans 'Threaten 1m Species with Extinction,'" BBC News, May 6, 2019, https://www.bbc.com/news/science-environment-48169783.

All of these habitats, living creatures, and life that make up our wonderful planet are at the mercy of those of us whose hands were designed to cultivate, care, and lift up. Unfortunately, our hands are often too pre-occupied with feeding our ever-increasing wants, building our kingdoms larger, and curating personal abundance. Often, instead of stewarding, we've over-consumed. Instead of caring for, we've colonized. Instead of loving, we've dominated. Might we confess that we've twisted our role here, making ourselves the center rather than the servant?

How do we respond to this as God's people? How do we step into the God-given creativity and Christlike dominion we are made for in order to be healing co-creators in this world?

To close this unit, it's fitting to return once more to God's relationality. Perhaps for too long we've allowed fear and the worry about pantheism (a belief that equates God with creation) to dictate our relationship with creation and inadvertently fuel a posture of domination in the world. Saint Francis of Assisi is an important member of our cloud of witnesses (see Hebrews 12:1) who has something to teach us about our relationship with the natural world. Written in 1224, this song by Saint Francis, known as "Canticle of the Creatures," is a beautiful composition reminding us that, as believers, we are called to be in special relationship with all of creation.

Canticle of the Creatures[6]

Most High, all-powerful, good Lord,
Yours are the praises, the glory, and the honour, and all blessing.

To you alone, Most High, do they belong,
and no human is worthy to mention your name.

Praised be you, my Lord, with all your creatures,
especially Sir Brother Sun,
Who is the day and through whom you give us light.

And he is beautiful and radiant with great splendour;
and bears a likeness of you, Most High One.

Praised be you, my Lord, through Sister Moon and the stars,
in heaven you formed them clear and precious and beautiful.

Praised be you, my Lord, through Brother Wind,
and through the air, cloudy and serene, and every kind of weather,
through whom you give sustenance to your creatures.

Praised be you, my Lord, through Sister Water,
who is very useful and humble and precious and chaste.

6. Text found at http://franciscanseculars.com/the-canticle-of-the-creatures.

Praised be you, my Lord, through Brother Fire,
through whom you light the night,
and he is beautiful and playful and robust and strong.

Praised be you, my Lord, through our Sister Mother Earth,
who sustains and governs us,
and who produces various fruit with coloured flowers and herbs.

Praised be you, my Lord, through those who give pardon for your
love, and bear infirmity and tribulation.

Blessed are those who endure in peace
for by you, Most High, shall they be crowned.

Praised be you, my Lord, through our Sister Bodily Death,
from whom no one living can escape.

Woe to those who die in mortal sin.
Blessed are those whom death will find in your most holy will,
for the second death shall do them no harm.

Praise and bless my Lord and give him thanks
and serve him with great humility.

REFLECT AND DISCUSS

- What new insights are sticking with you after reading through this unit?

- How have you noticed this creationivity and capacity for creation *within* creation before?

- Talk about being co-creators with God. What does this idea stir in you? How do you see yourself as a co-creator with God in the world?

- What are some of the ways you've noticed "dominion" and "subdue" interpreted as license to use creation as we please?

- How would it alter the way we consume if we viewed land, property, and other belongings as the Lord's instead of as ours?

- How could a practice of sabbath help us in our role of joining in the ongoing co-creation with God?

- What should be the response of the church today, as God's co-creators in the world, in the face of such environmental degradation?

- What causes you to grieve here? How might grief be the first appropriate response as the people of God?

- What inspires you from this unit? What energizes you?

- Spend time with your group discussing how the church might reengage in proper, Christlike, servant dominion with the world at large, and in your context locally.

RESPOND

Grow Outward

There's nothing quite like getting our hands in the dirt! One of the best first steps can be as easy as creating and growing a garden in your own backyard. Work with your community, small group, or family to adopt a natural area or plot of land that could become a pollinator garden, vegetable or herb garden, or butterfly waystation. This could be a grassy area around your church building or some area of your own neighborhood. For those in more urban spaces, start a container garden, or reclaim the stoop in front of your apartment. Use your collective voice and hands to embody caring dominion locally. How might you engage with the land in a life-giving, regenerative fashion that is good not only for you but also for the whole community?

Grow Inward

Do your own research into the state of our planet today. It's on us—since we are created to steward this common home of ours—to be familiar with and have the ability to speak about the environmental issues of our time. Visit NazarenesforCreationCare.com and click on the "Resources" tab to discover more.

Form a Green Habit

Track your carbon footprint! Visit FootprintCalculator.org and take the test to discover your personal carbon footprint level. Afterward, click on "Solutions" to explore different ways to reduce your personal carbon emissions. It might be through something as simple as automating your home-thermostat schedule, altering your diet, or planting more plants. There are also many helpful smartphone apps that help track your footprint and suggest lifestyle choices that you can change.

UNIT THREE
OUR FIRST VOCATION (GENESIS 2)

RYAN FASANI

ONE OF THE GREATEST GIFTS of my life was the grass field my parents sowed at my childhood home. Most kids I knew had a pool or treehouse or basketball hoop, but we were the only family that had a large grass field. We hosted volleyball tournaments, baseball practice, and soccer games; it was likely the most-used resource my family owned.

My greatest memories on that field, however, were not sports related. Before the ground was leveled, the irrigation installed, and the seeds planted, we had to contend with decomposed granite. In practical terms, that meant my parents needed topsoil—truckload upon truckload—before the ground would be hospitable for lawn seed germination and able to promote good root growth. For the better part of a year, dump trucks from local building sites discarded soil on our future soccer field. My parents were thankful for the free dirt—hundreds of cubic yards of a good growing medium—but my siblings and I were thankful for the temporary mountain range of raw material.

While my mom envisioned lush green grass, we begged to make the dirt mounds permanent. One day we wore army fatigues and built bunkers; the next day we made bike jumps; then we made an obstacle course. Every day was a new dirty adventure, and the possibilities seemed endless. Before it was a manicured ball field, it was something better: mounds of dirt, free to use how we wished.

Inherent in us all is an affinity for soil. Before concerns about time management and image, back when play was self-justified and stained clothes were acceptable, dirt piles, mud puddles, and sandy beaches were invitations to dream and create and roll around in. Are my childhood memories about a range of dirt piles mere nostalgia, or are they clues into an ancient truth about who we are created to be?

IN THE TEXT

This is the account of the heavens and the earth when they were created, when the LORD God made the earth and the heavens. Now no shrub had yet appeared on the earth and no plant had yet sprung up, for the LORD God had not sent rain on the earth and there was no one to work the ground.
—Genesis 2:4–5 (NIV)

Last unit we looked at Genesis 1:1–2, when God created heaven and earth. Here in Genesis 2, the creation story continues, but this time there's a different emphasis. What we commonly understand as "the fall," when humans first sinned, has not occurred yet in the story. I always thought that between the completion of creation and the fall, the world was a utopia that lacked nothing. Boy, was I wrong!

Genesis 2 opens by listing three matters that must be addressed. We read in verse 5 that foliage was lacking, water was in short supply, and there was a labor shortage. Of course, this was no surprise to the Creator. God immediately got to work addressing these three matters, as explained in verses 7–17.

First, God addressed the labor shortage: God saw "there was no one to work the ground" and wasted no time creating someone to help. God created *adam*, which is a Hebrew word that means "person" or "human." (A literal translation might be "earth being" or "earthling," in reference to our being formed from the dust of the ground, but we'll get to that.)

Second, in verses 8–9, God addressed the shortage of foliage by planting a garden. While the garden only gets two short verses, the narrative is keen to note that this was not merely ornamental vegetation, akin to a well-designed greenspace with a gravel path for lunchtime strolls. We might say God was the first farm-to-table gardener: God planted a garden that was "pleasing to the eye and good for food" (v. 9, NIV).

Now that the world had edible provisions and hands to tend it, God didn't leave the *adam* high and (literally) dry. Verses 10–15 recount how God addressed irrigation, the third issue. Instead of a light mist or fog, God employed the wisdom of a well-seasoned farmer: always install irrigation systems with future expansion in mind. God didn't create a stream to irrigate Eden alone; God created enough water for four rivers and a world of future gardens!

It's important to note that, while God addressed these three issues separately, they weren't independent of one another. God dealt with the issues presented early in this creation account by building an *inter-dependent system*. Quite brilliantly, the *adam* cared for the land, which in turn produced food for the *adam*; the river perpetually irrigated the vegetation, which in turn offered stability for its banks and natural purification; and, of course, the river hydrated the *adam* while the *adam* tended to and cared for the vegetation. At the center of God's creative problem solving was an affinity for sustainable ecological systems. God was the first gardener, and—like anyone who takes the craft of gardening seriously—God knew that each component of a garden is dependent on all the others. We will keep this in mind as we turn toward *how* God created humanity.

Then the LORD God formed a human from the dust of the ground and breathed into those nostrils the breath of life, and the human became a living being.
—Genesis 2:7 (author's translation)

God created humans, but God did not snap divine fingers and—poof!—a fully formed, 185-pound, male figure fell from the sky. No, the process was much more involved. God did not create from a distance, as Genesis 1 might suggest. Remember, God was the first gardener, and there is no such thing as absentee gardening. From cultivation to planting to weeding to harvesting, gardening requires intimate engagement with the natural world. It's slow, dirty work!

The story suggests that God created humans in the same way—up close and dirty. The "dust of the ground" in Hebrew is *adamah*, which literally means "the dirt of the earth," or "the soil under our feet." As we might expect of the world's first gardener, God took the *adamah* and formed the first *adam*. Did you catch that? God used the earth to make an *earth being*. (They even share the same root word!) But we're not made of only dirt. Humans are also made from the divine *ruach*, which means "breath" or "spirit." Without the breath of life, the first human was a human-like mass—all form, no vitality. Only with God's *ruach* are we given the necessary "ingredients" for life.

Remember that humans were God's solution to a need: the freshly minted world required a labor force. So God breathed God's very image into the soil. The implications are fascinating! Inherent in our being is the breath of creativity (see unit 2), an inclination to overcome challenges creatively, consonance with the life-giving Spirit, and a deep connection to the soil of the earth. Consider that for a moment: the first humans and, by extension, every human that followed, were intimately crafted by the divine Gardener with fresh soil and life-giving breath. We are an amalgamation of *soil* and *spirit*. It's no wonder we are drawn toward the dirt as children! My memory of dirt piles at my childhood home is not only nostalgia; it also points to a fundamental truth about creation: working and creating with dirt is rooted in our very being.

So if humanity is inclined to work with and play in the soil, then are we all supposed to be farmers? Yes and no. What we find in Genesis 2 may surprise you.

The Lord God took the human and put him in the
Garden of Eden to work it and take care of it.
—Genesis 2:15, author's translation

Immediately after addressing the irrigation need, God gave humanity its first task. As noted, God needed someone to work the ground (2:5), but God did not create humans to assign them just any work; rather, God uniquely created humans for a particular kind of work. This work assignment indicates a vocation, or calling, where God designates humans for a special function or task that they are uniquely prepared to accomplish. We see this truth at the heart of this creation account. God put the first humans in the garden of Eden to do two things: "till it and keep it." Truthfully, the English translation makes it seem mundane. The Hebrew is richer and more vitalizing. The words are *shamar*, literally meaning "to watch over, care for, and protect," and *abad*, "to work, tend, and cultivate."

What does it mean to watch over and protect land? What is so vitalizing about cultivating a plot of earth? *Protecting land* may not be what we first imagine. In many Western cultures, protection is often associated with self-defense and private property. Protecting land in those contexts means demarcating boundaries, placing pins in the corners of plots, and building fences. In Genesis 2, protecting means something different; it connotes sincere concern for the well-being of the other. *Shamar* is less about defining and defending what's ours and more about developing a close enough relationship with the natural world for which we are responsible that at all times we know its needs intimately and care for it passionately! Another way to say it is this: watching over and protecting land is a call to be in relationship with the land, attending to its needs and being aware of its vulnerabilities.

How about working, tending, cultivating land? The Hebrew word *abad* has very little correlation to modern-day farming that's done from atop massive John Deere tractors. Part of what *abad* means does refer to the type of farm work most of us are familiar with, at least in concept if not in practice: turning the soil for seed, digging a hole for a tree, or cutting a trench for bulbs. But the other part of the meaning is fascinating because it's about *service*. We can't deny that *abad* indicates hard work, which all cultivation and gardening entails. But the call to cultivate the soil comes with an expectation that the human will do it with a spirit of humility and love. This is why the noun form of the word *abad* (*ebed*) can be translated "servant." The first human was expected to *serve* the health of the soil. In good ecological fashion, life is a balanced cycle: the soil (*adamah*) first gives of itself to form humans (*adam*), and now humans are charged with giving of themselves to assure the life of the soil. We are composed of life-giving soil, and we give life back *to* the soil.

If our original calling is to work and take care of the land, does that mean everyone is meant to be a farmer? Not by trade, no. But there is an implication that stewarding land—being intimately aware of its needs and in humble service to its well-being—remains a central priority for all humans.

IN OUR WORLD TODAY

At either end of the food chain you find a biological system—
a patch of soil, a human body—and the health of one is connected—
literally—to the health of the other.
—Michael Pollan[1]

Humanity's first vocation was to work the land and care for it—that is, they were called to lovingly care for all the life that was sustained on that *one piece of land*. I'd like to propose a way for us to follow in their vocational footsteps, but first, I need to make an explicit connection that surely would not have been missed by the early hearers of this creation story.

1. Michael Pollan, *The Omnivore's Dilemma: A Natural History of Four Meals* (New York: Penguin Random House, 2006), 9.

Foragers, hunters and gatherers, and farmers—anyone who lives close to the land—know in their bones what scientists have verified in the last hundred years: the health of the land affects the health of humanity. To be more direct, the health of the soil literally determines the health of our bodies. We are what we eat. Many of us who "harvest" food off shelves and transport it to our vehicles in shopping carts might miss what was obvious to an ancient audience: the soil (*adamah*) used to form the first human (*adam*) is the same soil that sustains humanity and, in turn, is the soil humanity is called to love and care for.

Wendell Berry, a writer and longtime champion of small farms, local economies, and sustainable agricultural practices, argues for the same principles we've discovered in this creation story. Namely, we are all only one or two steps removed from cultivated soil. For supermarket patrons, a direct connection to the cultivated soil may seem ludicrous, especially for those who steer clear of the produce section, where "naked" fruits and vegetables appear in all their glory. However, those bagged tortilla chips are made primarily of corn and salt. Corn was grown by a farmer. Salt was harvested by a farmer too. And the salsa you ate with it: almost every ingredient was planted, grown, and picked by a farmer. Even foods as obscure as a Twinkie or Ritz crackers are full of ingredients that were grown in the ground. This is why one of Berry's often-quoted contentions is, "Eating is an agricultural act."[2]

---

2. Wendell Berry, "The Pleasures of Eating," *What Are People For? Essays* (New York: North Point Press, 1990), 145–152.

Humans all over the earth live in different environments and have varying levels of access to land. But *we all eat!* Rural or urban, real estate agent or schoolteacher—every single one of us, one or two or three times per day, turns nature into culture, turns the body of the world into a human body. At each meal we are reliving the creation story of *building physical bodies with soil.*

One of my jobs is market gardening, which basically means I grow a lot of food in a small amount of space. Without debate, soil fertility is the most important resource for maximizing production. I've learned three principles in the last ten years for maintaining soil health: (1) never leave soil bare, (2) minimize the disruption of the microbiology, and (3) diversify and rotate crops.

Unfortunately, these three principles are nearly universally ignored by industrial agriculture—the very system that likely grew the ingredients for those tortilla chips and Twinkies. It is standard practice for what we call "Big Ag" to level native, diverse ground cover and replace it with row crops and orchards or massive beef operations. What once was a nutrient-replenishing, protected ecosystem becomes mostly exposed to the elements, promoting erosion and leaching. Further, it is standard practice for these large-scale farms to employ mono-cropping. As the name implies, large swaths of land are committed to singular or limited crop growth, ignoring anything we find in nature. Despite the appeal of standardization and efficiency, mono-cropping makes crops susceptible to disease and disproportionately taxes and depletes some of the soil's nutrients. It's no surprise that largely exposed land covered in a single crop results in increasing pest pressure and diminishing returns. The industrial solution for this industrial agricultural problem has become pesticide and fertilizer. Unfortunately, these remedies help plants appear healthy above ground in the short term but are disastrous in the long run for the microorganisms below the ground. These petro-chemicals destroy the very subterranean workhorses that convert organic matter in the soil into usable nutrients for plants.

Adam and Eve were called to work and take care of the land because all life on that land—including their own—depended on their loving care of the soil. So how do we follow in Adam and Eve's vocational footsteps?

Keep eating! (That seems easy enough.) Remember, eating is an agricultural act, which means every morsel of food we consume either stewards the land in the spirit of our first vocational call, or it doesn't. Soil is the foundation of every farm, and by extension it's the foundation of every food system, every society, and every human. If we neglect its health, we neglect the very basis for the health of our own bodies and all creation. We are called to work and take care of the land because, in doing so, we are ensuring access to the means of abundant life.

REFLECT AND DISCUSS

- What is the most surprising thing you learned about creation in Genesis 2?

- What memories do you have of playing outside or in the dirt as a child?

- How do you feel drawn (or not drawn) to the land now?

- What are the implications of the fact that "human" (*adam*) and "soil" (*adamah*) share the same Hebrew root?

- How can people who are not directly involved in agriculture or farming care for the soil today?

- What human activities harm soil? What changes can we make to turn this around on a personal or social level?

- Why does the creation story highlight dirt, vegetation, and the ecosystem of Eden?

- What comes to mind when you hear the phrase "till it and keep it" from Genesis 2:15? Stewardship? Intimacy? Gentle, loving care? Why or why not?

- What experiences have you had in the connection between soil and bodily health?

- Discuss the practical implications of Wendell Berry's statement: *Eating is an agricultural act.* How might we eat in a way that is faithful to our original calling and promotes the health of the soil and our bodies?

- How does it make you feel to hear that humanity is called to care for the land? Inspired? Intimidated? Something else?

- How can a church take seriously its call to land-and-soil stewardship?

RESPOND

Grow Outward

There's nothing quite like being in nature to grow our awareness of the natural world and develop a care for its needs. Make a monthly, weekly, or even daily commitment to go on a walk outdoors. Stroll through a local park, along a riverbank, or through a green space near your work, and do it at a pace that is intentionally slow. Take in the scents, listen closely for the native sounds, and look for movements, textures, and colors that are only found outside. Look for evidence of an interconnected ecosystem. Perhaps rotting logs have become a habitat for squirrels and mice or fallen leaves are building the next generation of topsoil. Maybe there is a stream that irrigates vegetation? Incorporate a simple prayer on your walk, something like: *Creator God, all of this flourishing begins with the soil; help me see ways I can contribute to its health.*

Grow Inward

We are formed from soil from the beginning. It is in us, along with God's very breath. Attempt to develop a better understanding of yourself by finding a resource to help you learn about the fascinating complexities of soil. Nurture growth in the Spirit by investigating the numerous connections between soil health and the physiological well-being of humans and human societies at large. Begin to directly engage your original responsibility to steward land by ordering a few seeds—any seeds will do, though wildflowers are the easiest—and tuck them in the soil near your home. (Maybe there *is* a little farmer in each of us after all!)

Form a Green Habit

Wendell Berry insisted that eating is an agricultural act and therefore is directly related to soil management. The closest some of us can come to our original calling is to eat in a way that supports the flourishing of land and the surrounding ecosystems. A new green habit could be to meet and support a local farmer who has devoted their life to soil health. This is easier now more than ever. Attend a local farmers' market. It's very likely that every farmer there is stewarding land. Introduce yourself, inquire about their farm, and take home a bag full of delicious produce.

UNIT FOUR

REDISCOVERING GOD'S LIMITS

(GENESIS 3)

MEGAN M. PARDUE

PARENTS SPEND a significant amount of child-raising time setting limits and boundaries. It starts early, from the moment children begin to move on their own. We put up gates, cover electrical outlets, and check floors for tiny objects that could end up in the mouth. As children grow and gain independence, we teach new boundaries for continued safety: the stove is hot; look both ways before crossing the street; don't play with matches.

My kids love to ride their bikes and scooters on a long, paved trail near our house. I let them ride ahead of me until I catch up on foot. It's one of our favorite things to do together, and they know the boundaries on our well-traveled route. They ride from the start of the trail to the first bend. Then they stop and wait for Mom. Once I've caught them at the bend, they cruise to the bottom of the bridge. Then they stop and wait again. After the bridge, it's the green bench on the left. Then the purple sign. Then the parking meter. When we get to the end of the trail, their adventures ahead of me end. Traffic increases. We have to cross busy streets. In the city, we all stick together.

Adults also live with limits and boundaries. I limit how late I stay up if I have an early morning the next day. I set boundaries in relationships in order for them to stay healthy. As I get older, my body can only tolerate a small amount of sugar, or I quickly feel lousy and lethargic, so I try to limit how much I eat. Even as we live within limits and boundaries, we hear a contradictory story. This story has many variations, but it sounds something like this: *The sky's the limit. You can do or be whatever you want. If you work hard, you'll make a lot of money.*

These realities are only true for some people. It's actually not a level playing field in the workplace, especially for women and people of color. But even aside from the historical patterns of discrimination and marginalization, there are still plenty of people who can't do or be whatever they want. Diagnoses happen. Unexpected losses occur. Disasters strike. Even though most of us know this to be true, "the sky's the limit" story of growth, especially as it relates to wealth and the accumulation of possessions, has a remarkably strong grip on our ways of seeing and living in the world.

Is this what God desires for us? The accumulation of material possessions? The storing up of treasures on earth? Or does God have another way—one with limits and boundaries?

IN THE TEXT

In the last unit, we took a close look at soil and the role God gave Adam and Eve to tend the garden with care. In this unit we read one additional instruction that God gave to Adam.

> *And the LORD God commanded the man, "You are free to eat from any tree in the garden; but you must not eat*

from the tree of the knowledge of good and evil, for when
you eat from it you will certainly die."
—Genesis 2:16–17 (NIV)

Our unit this week feels like it drops us into the middle of a day's work. Imagine Eve kneeling in the dirt, nestling small seeds into their new home in the ground. Adam is doing the same on the other side of the row. While they work near the orchard, the serpent interrupts their quiet focus with a question.

Now the serpent was more crafty than any of the wild animals the LORD God had made. He said to the woman, "Did God really say, 'You must not eat from any tree in the garden'?"

The woman said to the serpent, "We may eat fruit from the trees in the garden, but God did say, 'You must not eat fruit from the tree that is in the middle of the garden, and you must not touch it, or you will die.'"

"You will not certainly die," the serpent said to the woman. "For God knows that when you eat from it your eyes will be opened, and you will be like God, knowing good and evil."
—Genesis 3:1–5 (NIV)

"Did God *really* say that? Are you sure?" While Eve and Adam were sowing seeds that would produce fruit, the serpent started sowing the seeds of doubt. *Don't you want to be like God, knowing good and evil? Who wouldn't want to be like God? Limitless? Without boundaries? All-powerful? All-knowing? Don't you want everything to be yours?*

It's so easy to fault Eve and Adam for falling to this temptation. God gave them one limit in the whole garden. One boundary! How could it be so hard? We are, as we have discussed already, made in God's image and likeness. The serpent wasn't tempting Eve and Adam to acknowledge the ways in which they are created in the image of God, for they already knew their belovedness, and they had no shame. The serpent was tempting them to desire to *be* God—or at least be *equal* to God in knowledge, limitlessness, and power.

It seems that so much of the environmental crises we face today stem from a similar temptation: we too want to be God. That may sound extreme. I doubt anyone reading this woke up this morning thinking, *I wish I could be God today and live without limits!* But many of us (especially in the Western world and the global North) live on the earth as if there *are* no limits to our consumption, no consequences for our actions, and no repercussions for our excessive use of resources. We want more. We love growth. We want our incomes to grow, our churches to grow, our businesses to grow, the size of our home to grow, the size of our bank accounts to grow. *More, faster, stronger, sooner, easier.*

My guess is that some of us have never considered the problems with our growth-without-limits mindset. It's not a desire we *intended* to adopt or accept. For many of us, the desire for more or the desire to grow is ingrained in us because of our culture. The world we live in—including some of our churches—has planted and nurtured these desires in us from an early age. Everything, from advertising to ideologies, reinforces the desire for more without limits.

Eve and Adam didn't begin their day of work with a plan to eat the fruit. Similarly, we didn't set out to be captive to a limitless desire for more. But, like the serpent said, *Did God really say that you should tend the garden and not dominate the earth?* We hear similar whispers toward limitless consumption: *Are you sure you don't need a bigger house? Are you sure you don't want to give your kids or grandkids the best Christmas they've ever had? Do you really need to consider the way that choice would impact the earth?*

When the woman saw that the fruit of the tree was good for food and pleasing to the eye, and also desirable for gaining wisdom, she took some and ate it. She also gave some to her husband, who was with her, and he ate it. Then the eyes of both of them were opened, and

they realized they were naked; so they sewed fig leaves
together and made coverings for themselves.
—*Genesis 3:6–7 (NIV)*

Eve and Adam crossed the boundary that God set for them. (Notice that the scripture is very clear. Artistic depictions and retellings often leave Adam out of the scene entirely, but he was right there with her!) They consumed the forbidden fruit that the serpent promised would open their eyes and make them like God, knowing good and evil. With their newly open eyes, they realized they were naked and made clothes for themselves. Once they had their eyes opened, there was no turning back. As the saying goes, "You can't *unsee* that."

This part of the story offers an interlude for reflection in our study. By now, in unit four, I hope you have had your eyes opened to new ways of understanding these chapters in Genesis and also to the essential connections between being a child of God and caring for creation. Our attention to and love of God's creation are as intricately tied to our faith and life of discipleship as other practices, such as prayer and fasting. Many of us may be seeing these connections for the first time. Others have identified some of the ways we are actively harming the earth. Much like Eve and Adam, our eyes have been opened. There's no turning back. We can't unsee these connections we're making. What is God stirring within you today?

To Adam he said, "Because you listened to your wife
and ate fruit from the tree about which I commanded
you, 'You must not eat from it,' Cursed is the ground
because of you; through painful toil you will eat food
from it all the days of your life. It will produce thorns
and thistles for you, and you will eat the plants of the
field. By the sweat of your brow you will eat your food
until you return to the ground, since from it you were
taken; for dust you are and to dust you will return."
—Genesis 3:17–19 (NIV)

Because you ate the fruit . . .

Many of us speak of sin as something abstract or something that happens in our minds and hearts rather than something that has concrete,
tangible consequences. But look at the specific language in Genesis 3
around earth and physical bodies: *animals, dust, pain, labor, ground,*
toil, thorns, thistles, plants, field, sweat, brow, garments, tree. Violating
the limit has real, material consequences. "Because you ate the fruit"
matters—materially and concretely—for Eve, for Adam, and even for
the serpent. Since we are humans, we tend to focus on what changes for Eve and Adam as a result of their sin: the sweat of their brows

while working the land, pain in childbirth, and ultimately death (their return to dust). We also focus on the way their relationship with God is altered, since God requires them to leave the garden and live outside of paradise.

But notice that not only does their boundary crossing have consequences for humanity and for humanity's relationship with God; their choice actually *also* impacts the earth itself. "Cursed is the ground because of you. . . . It will produce thorns and thistles for you" (vv. 17, 18). What a significant shift in our understanding of sin. How many of us have considered the way our limitless living impacts the earth?

Right now the earth is experiencing the measurable consequences of human activity. Changes in our atmosphere, weather, and climate impact land, water, animals, and yes, people too. Overconsumption, overuse, and our addiction to limitless living play a huge part in contributing to these changes. What makes matters worse is that the impacts of these changes—heat waves, flooding, and poor air quality, to name a few—disproportionately affect people who are already poor, people without insurance, nonwhite people, and people without the resources to move away from a disaster zone or to rebuild after disaster strikes.[1] There are hundreds of thousands of such people in our global family who haven't had the luxury of living without limits—which

---

1. "EPA Report Shows Disproportionate Impacts of Climate Change on Socially Vulnerable Populations in the United States," United States Environmental Protection Agency, September 2, 2021, https://www.epa.gov/newsreleases/epa-report-shows-disproportionate-impacts-climate-change-socially-vulnerable.

means they and their communities have done little or nothing to cause the changes that so negatively impact them today.[2]

God has another way for us. It is the way that Eve and Adam rejected, but we can learn from their mistake and begin living within reasonable limits again. We can examine the hold that the growth mindset has on us, perhaps for the first time. We can set limits for ourselves and for our communities and begin living into those limits. While we are prone to forget, we are already a people with limits. For those in my faith community, look at what our church expects of us:

> The Church of the Nazarene believes this new and holy way of life involves practices to be avoided and redemptive acts of love to be accomplished for the souls, minds, and bodies of our neighbors. One redemptive arena of love involves the special relationship Jesus had, and commanded his disciples to have, with the poor of this world; *that his church ought, first, to keep itself simple and free from an emphasis on wealth and extravagance and, second, to give itself to the care, feeding, clothing, and shelter of the poor and marginalized.* Throughout the Bible and in the life and example of Jesus, God identifies with and assists the poor, the oppressed, and those in society who cannot speak for themselves. In the same way, we, too, are called to identify with and to enter into solidarity with the

---

2. Laura Paddison, "How the Rich Are Driving Climate Change," BBC, October 27, 2021, https://www.bbc.com/future/article/20211025-climate-how-to-make-the-rich-pay-for-their-carbon-emissions.

poor. We hold that compassionate ministry to the poor includes acts of charity as well as a struggle to provide opportunity, equality, and justice for the poor. We further believe the Christian's responsibility to the poor is an essential aspect of the life of every believer who seeks a faith that works through love. We believe Christian holiness to be inseparable from ministry to the poor in that it drives the Christian beyond their own individual perfection and toward the creation of a more just and equitable society and world. Holiness, far from distancing believers from the desperate economic needs of people in this world, motivates us to place our means in the service of alleviating such need and to adjust our wants in accordance with the needs of others.[3]

Our relationship with creation directly impacts those who are poor, oppressed, and marginalized. Now is the time to open our eyes.

IN OUR WORLD TODAY

One of the significant challenges of exploring our limitless living, evidenced by overconsumption and overuse of natural resources, is just how overwhelming and numerous the problems are. Let's narrow our scope and take a focused look at trees, which are literally "trees of life" for us today. The mass destruction of trees—deforestation—occurs for a vari-

---

3. "Part III, The Covenant of Christian Conduct, A. The Christian Life, 28.3," *Church of the Nazarene Manual: 2017–2021* (Kansas City, MO: Nazarene Publishing House, 2017), 46–47.

ety of reasons, but most link back to our limitless living. Since 1990, the world has lost about a billion acres of forest, according to the Food and Agricultural Organization of the United Nations. It's hard to wrap our minds around that kind of loss. Much of the loss is due to farming, grazing of livestock, drilling, and mining. Logging—the practice of cutting down trees to produce everything from lumber to paper to cardboard boxes for two-day shipping—is another major cause of deforestation. As urban sprawl continues, more trees are cut down to make way for new housing developments and even new church buildings.[4]

Deforestation is an environmental nightmare, and here's one reason why. Among their other valuable environmental contributions like clean air, animal habitats, and remarkable beauty, trees absorb and store carbon, along with heat-trapping greenhouse gases that human activities emit. When trees are cut down, those gases they were storing are released into the atmosphere, contributing to the warming of our planet. A warmer planet increases conditions for the record-breaking forest fires we've begun to see in our lifetime. When more trees burn due to uncontrolled wildfires, then even more previously absorbed warming gases release into the atmosphere, perpetuating and worsening a vicious cycle.[5]

4. Christina Nunez, "Climate 101: Deforestation," *National Geographic*, https://www.nationalgeographic.com/environment/article/deforestation/.

5. Jake Horton and Daniele Palumbo, "Europe Wildfires: Are They Linked to Climate Change?" BBC News, July 21, 2022, https://www.bbc.com/news/58159451.

In North Carolina and other coastal communities in the United States and around the world, forests are dying for a different reason. As the earth warms, ice caps melt, sea levels rise, and saltwater seeps into previously healthy soil near the coastlands, functionally poisoning the soil and drowning the trees. These trees die without ever being cut down, so they are no longer able to absorb and store carbon like we desperately need them to do. Their stumps stand limbless and bare, ghosts of a previously vibrant forest. The destruction on the North Carolina coast is so significant that the changes over the last thirty-five years can be seen in satellite imagery from space.[6]

You will go out in joy and be led forth in peace; the mountain and hills will burst into song before you, and all the trees of the field will clap their hands. Instead of the thornbush will grow the juniper, and instead of briers the myrtle will grow. This will be for the LORD's renown, for an everlasting sign, that will endure forever.
—Isaiah 55:12–13 (NIV)

6. Robin A. Smith, "Mapping North Carolina's Ghost Forests from 430 Miles Up," *Duke Today*, April 5, 2021, https://today.duke.edu/2021/04/mapping-north-carolinas-ghost-forests-430-miles.

The trees of the field will clap their hands? The mountains and hills burst into songs of praise? Who are we to keep creation from saying glory to God? Who are we to silence the song of the trees? We desperately need limits and boundaries for our consumption. There are measurable consequences for our actions and repercussions for our excessive use of resources. Just look at the trees! But God and God's community have another way for us to live: confessing our wrong-headed love for limitless living, rejecting the "sky's the limit" mindset for more, and evaluating our addiction to growth. Most of us have enough already.

For centuries, Christians have marked the beginning of the season of Lent with a service called Ash Wednesday. In this time of worship, the pastor marks the forehead of each person with ashes that are the result of burning the previous year's Palm Sunday branches. As pastors mark the foreheads with ash, they repeat something close to what Eve and Adam heard in the garden that day: *From dust you were formed, and to dust you shall return.* In hearing these words and being marked with dust, we remember that God created us from dust, and we are reminded of the fragility of life and of the limits of the time we have.

The poet Malcom Guite reflects on this Christian practice and the crises of our planet in the sonnet "Ash Wednesday."

Ash Wednesday

Receive this cross of ash upon your brow,
Brought from the burning of Palm Sunday's cross.
The forests of the world are burning now
And you make late repentance for the loss.
But all the trees of God would clap their hands
The very stones themselves would shout and sing
If you could covenant to love these lands
And recognise in Christ their Lord and King.

He sees the slow destruction of those trees,
He weeps to see the ancient places burn,
And still you make what purchases you please,
And still to dust and ashes you return.
But Hope could rise from ashes even now
Beginning with this sign upon your brow.[7]

7. Malcolm Guite, "Ash Wednesday," March 2, 2022, https://malcolmguite.wordpress.com/2022/03/02/a-sonnet-for-ash-wednesday-6/.

REFLECT AND DISCUSS

- Name some of the ways that many of us behave as if our resources are unlimited. Be specific. If you are struggling to come
  up with examples, consider your day yesterday:

  o Where did you wake up? If in your own home, how much
    energy was expended overnight while you slept? (Consider
    HVAC units, fans, nightlights, charging phones, security/
    alarm systems, plugged-in appliances, etc.)

  o How did you travel to the places you went yesterday?

  o What did you eat? Where did your food come from?

- How much of a hold does the growth mindset have on you?

- What in this unit has made you feel uncomfortable?

- What in this unit has inspired you?

- What are some of the ways that our culture shapes us to desire more?

- Name two or three ways your eyes have been opened in our study up to this point.

- What are some of the ways that human actions impact the earth?

- Is simplicity a regular part and consideration of your church's life together?

  o If so, discuss whether it's by intentional choice or by necessity (e.g., budget concerns are a necessity, not a creation-care choice).

  o If not, how can your church community practice setting limits on wealth, spending, or extravagance?

- Spend time with your group discussing how you might reengage in living with limits, both as individuals and as a community.

RESPOND

Grow Outward

Take a look at the trees where you live. Perhaps they are in your own yard. Perhaps they are planted in a grassy median or a park near your home. Can you identify what kind of trees they are? If not, do your best to find out what they are. Find out who is committed to planting trees in your community. Do they need volunteers? Do they have the local support they need from the county or city? Can you plant trees on your church property that could become carbon stores for future generations? Make a tree-planting plan!

Grow Inward

Do a thoughtful and prayerful evaluation of the hold that limitless living and the growth mindset have on you. Spend a week journaling, examining, and prayerfully considering how captive you've been to this mindset. Where does it come up for you? How has it shaped you? How can you resist it starting now?

Form a Green Habit

Consider giving up shopping for anything that isn't food or toiletries. Start small. Try it for three days, a week, two weeks, a month. What did you notice during the time you stopped shopping? How difficult or easy was it? Once you begin shopping again, consider a set of test questions to help you evaluate purchases more intentionally. Here are some suggestions:

- Keep a list on a piece of paper, on your phone, or in an online shopping cart of nonessential things you want to purchase. Leave the list alone for two weeks. When you check back in with your list, consider whether you still want the items listed or if you can live fine without them.

- Before you purchase something new, ask yourself the following:

  o Can I borrow it?

  o Can I make it?

  o Can I buy it used or secondhand?

  o Can I repair or fix what I have?

  o Can I buy it locally or from a small business to keep money in my community and limit the packaging and waste that comes with online ordering?

I AM WE
(GENESIS 4)

TODD WOMACK

AS MUCH AS I LOVE the city of Flint, Michigan, I have an even deeper love for my second home in Magee, Mississippi. Both of my parents were born and raised in Magee, where they came from humble beginnings. On my mother's side, I am the great-great grandson of a slave owner. My mother grew up without modern amenities like electricity, gas, and running water. Visits to my grandmother and grandfather years later reminded us that they still lived this frugal life without modern conveniences. Candles and kerosene lanterns provided light. The home was heated by a wood-burning stove, and one of my chores when we visited was to go outside and chop wood in order to keep the stove burning.

I have fonder memories of the water-collection ritual at my grandparents' house. My grandfather had discovered a running spring about a mile away from the house, located deep down in the woods. The only way we could get there was by the landmarks my grandfather taught us to identify. We exited out the back of the house and looked for the big, dark oak tree. Once we found the oak tree, we looked for the crooked path. We followed the crooked path to the barbed-wire fence and beyond, until we came to a drop-off. From the drop-off, we looked for the three dark rocks that marked the source of the spring. Climbing down, we moved the rocks, then the flat wooden board, and finally the cloth that revealed a square tin box my grandfather had driven into the ground so the water would flow up to the brim. We looked at the abundant spring water in amazement, like children looking into the window of a candy store. "We found it!" we would say as we smiled and laughed together. After our brief celebration we took turns drinking the cool, revivifying spring water from the ladle my grandfather had hidden there.

Only by working together could we find that spring. At an early age we recognized that the journey was collective in the same way that the water itself was for all. I had never tasted anything so refreshing and life-giving as the water that came from that spring. I marveled at how nature could produce such a gift and how this cool water was coming from the red-clay ground in the middle of some woods in Mississippi! To this day, no cool drink of water I have ever experienced has come close to the taste of that spring water.

In this unit we'll look at and talk about what it means to view community from a faith-based perspective, considering the idea that we are all interconnected, both to other humans and to the earth that God has created. We will reflect on the concepts of environmental racism, commodification, and *ubuntu*. We will also begin to examine issues related to individualism and collectivism. Finally, we will discover what it means to view God's creation within the concept of community and what is needed to move forward as a *community* of believers.

IN THE TEXT

Then the LORD *said to Cain, "Where is your*
brother Abel?" He said, "I do not know;
am I my brother's keeper?"
—*Genesis 4:9 (NRSVUE)*

This familiar passage focuses on the relationship between God and two of Adam and Eve's children, Cain and his brother Abel. God's open-ended question to Cain about where Abel was attempted to elicit a narrative response from Cain. God could have easily asked Cain, "Did you kill your brother Abel?" or even, "*Why* did you kill your brother Abel?"—but he didn't. Cain was free to answer openly, with no limitations. God gave Cain the opportunity to give an answer that addressed what, who, when, where and why. God the Father offered Cain the chance to go deeper, to explain, maybe even to express remorse over the loss of his brother and to provide God the opportunity to teach him about compassion. Ultimately, God's question was an act of mercy and love that provided Cain with a safe space to share his heart, to be vulnerable, and to be transparent and honest with God. Cain's choice to answer God's question with a question makes it appear as though Cain wanted to avoid accountability for his choices—a pattern of brokenness comparable to his parents' decision to hide their nakedness in the bushes in Genesis 3.

It's crucial to note that when Cain asked, "Am I my brother's keeper?" he was using the same term found in Genesis 2:15, *shamar*, "to keep, guard, protect, care for." Cain's vocation as a farmer was revealed in Genesis 4:2, where he was described as a "tiller" or "servant" (*abad*, also found in 2:15) of the ground, *adamah*. Apparently Cain knew that his responsibility was to "keep" or "care for" the land, but in his excuses to God he attempted to narrow this responsibility to his farming only, not extending it to his brother. Cain's response could be expressed as, "My job is to keep the ground, not my brother!"

This perspective brings God's response all the more into focus. God responded to Cain's question by saying in 4:10 (NIV), "Listen! Your brother's blood cries out to me from the ground [*adamah*]."[1] God reconnected what Cain attempted to separate—care for the land and care for his brother. Fittingly, Cain's punishment was brokenness and separation from the ground (vv. 11–12). Cain's jealousy, anger, and disdain toward Abel and his greed for God's attention caused him to treat his brother's life as something that could be possessed, taken, and disposed of to get what he wanted.

Cain was the first to leverage human life for personal gain. Sin always attempts to segregate like this. It's an eerily familiar story for us as we think about all the ways we've marginalized others, intentionally or unintentionally, for our own benefit. It should come as no surprise that in the end we find that, when our neighbors are oppressed, so are we.

1. See unit 3.

Today we often fail to recognize that there is not an "us" and a "creation." Humans are part of creation—that is, we are *the rest of creation*! People and nature are not separate. God's creation is one. Often we use this error of separating humans from nature to justify our exploitation of the earth for some temporary economic benefit for a few. At other times, as was the case with Cain, the separation of people from creation results in a disregard for human life, which happens when we fail to understand that it is not either/or when it comes to matters of caring for people and the proper care of God's creation. We tend to forget that exploiting creation for temporary economic gain will hurt not only nature but also our human brothers and sisters—around the world *and* next door! As it happens, we actually *are* our "brother's keeper."

IN OUR WORLD TODAY

Unfortunately, the story of that spring on my grandparents' land doesn't have a happy ending. The flow of the spring was eventually disrupted due to loggers coming through and cutting down the trees and trampling the land. The tin box my grandfather built to collect life-sustaining water for his family is now forever empty. When I think about this I am both grieved and angered. The land my grandfather owned is now being stripped for its timber for the sake of distant people who had no idea that a hidden, life-sustaining spring was even there. Unfortunately, because of the harsh realities of our world's racial-historical context, I have sometimes wondered if this violation of creation and the gift of water would have taken place if the land had been owned by a person of European ancestry rather than a person of African ancestry.

The story about my grandfather's freshwater spring raises a question for all of us: What role does race play in sorting out land use?[2] Did you know that race is the most significant predictor of whether a person lives near contaminated soil, air, and water? As a matter of fact, "people of color are two times more likely to live without potable water and modern sanitation."[3] This reality is called environmental racism: "Environmental racism refers to any policy, practice, or directive that differentially affects or disadvantages (whether intended or unintended) individuals, groups, or communities based on race or color."[4] This kind of racism may not be deliberate or conscious, but it exists nevertheless and is most clearly evident in the tendency to exploit the environment or locate toxic waste dumps in neighborhoods not inhabited by the privileged—which, in Euro-American cultures, includes the white middle classes and above.

The sobering fact is that racism often manifests itself most obviously in the allocation of scarce resources, particularly water. It's the age-old Cain and Abel story all over again—one person or group exploiting

2. Robert D. Bullard, *Dumping In Dixie: Race, Class, and Environmental Quality* (New York: Taylor & Francis, 1994).

3. Bryce Covert, "Race Best Predicts Whether You Live Near Pollution: Environmental Racism Extends Far beyond Flint," *The Nation* (February 2016), https://www.thenation.com/article/archive/race-best-predicts-whether-you-live-near-pollution/.

4. Bullard, *Dumping in Dixie*, 98.

their sisters and brothers in order to gain something for themselves. We are created to look after one another when it comes to the rest of God's creation. No one's zip code, ethnicity, skin color, nationality, gender identity, sexual orientation, age, or any other factor should have any impact on their access to God's gift of the earth's natural resources, and specifically water. The issue of access to water is near and dear to my heart because I was born and raised in the city of Flint, Michigan. In Flint, we locals lovingly refer to such people as "Flintstones." Flint's water problems have become infamous and have been widely reported in the media.[5]

It's no wonder Flint's water crisis drew such attention, since no nutrient is more critical to life—or more taken for granted—than water. I became abruptly aware of the problem of water's availability years ago, when I was in the Marines and on leave in San Diego, California. While walking in the neighborhoods on a hot night, my fellow Marines and I became thirsty but could not find a water fountain anywhere. Then we saw something in the middle of an alley—not a water fountain but a vending machine selling bottled water. I was taken aback and stated forcefully, "I will never pay for water!" In my mind, water should be a natural and free resource that all deserve equal access to. This experience was my baptism (no pun intended) into the idea of commodification of water and, more importantly, the exploitation of God's gift to humankind.

---

5. Michael Ray, "Flint Water Crisis," *Encyclopedia Britannica*, September 2022, https://www.britannica.com/event/Flint-water-crisis.

Water is the source of all life. In the Genesis 1 poem of creation, we find that water is already present in the second verse even before God's creating work gets underway: "the earth was complete chaos, and darkness covered the face of the deep, while a wind from God swept over the face of the waters" (NRSVUE). Water is truly essential for all life and shouldn't be withheld from any creature. Access to clean water is quickly becoming one of the most pressing global social justice issues in our time. The United Nations names water as a human right, which entitles "everyone to sufficient, safe, acceptable and physically accessible, and affordable water for personal and domestic uses."[6]

Writer and activist Lydia Wylie-Kellermann states, "Water, which is neither renewable nor infinite, is in danger. Our capitalist, consumer, entitlement economies and lifestyles have perpetrated great violence on the waters, leaving a bleeding earth and our future in danger. Polluted and commodified, water has become the next battleground for corporate grabs, military conflict, and occupation."[7] Water—God's free gift to all God's creation—has been wrongfully turned into a commodity. Viewed in this way, water is assigned economic value, which in turn gives it a commercial value.

6. "The Human Right to Water and Sanitation," United Nations Department of Economic and Social Affairs, https://www.un.org/waterforlifedecade/human_right_to_water.shtml.

7. Lydia Wylie-Kellermann, "Wild Lectionary: God's Gonna Trouble the Waters," *Radical Discipleship*, February 2018, https://radicaldiscipleship.net/2018/02/15/wild-lectionary-gods-gonna-trouble-the-waters/.

Today, there are both global and local inequalities surrounding who can access clean water and who can't—and these inequalities often have little to do with the availability of nearby water. When we speak of water scarcity, the most salient issues are lack of water, accessibility of water to the poor, ownership and control, commercialization, and governance and development. The corporate sins that have been committed in relation to water have led to two unfortunate results: (1) whoever can pay the most gets access to resources and (2) private ownership undermines public rights.

In my home state of Michigan, we have more *access* to drinkable, fresh water than any other place in the world! However, in my dear city of Flint in 2015, water rates were "almost eight times higher than the national average."[8] This rate was three times higher than just down the road in Detroit! In 2015, Detroit residents were typically paying approximately $249 annually for water, whereas Flint residents paid approximately $864. The United Nations designates affordable water and sewer services to be about 3 percent of household income. Flint's percentage in 2015 was at 7 percent. What may simply look like high water bills and bad luck on the surface were in fact indicators of something much more broken underneath.

---

8. Ron Fonger, "Flint Water Prices Almost Eight Times National Average, Erin Brockovich Associate Says," *MLive*, March 2015, https://www.mlive.com/news/flint/2015/03/erin_brockovich_associate_says.html.

The crisis in Flint came to a head in 2014, when a state-appointed emergency city manager changed the city's water supply from Detroit's water system to the Flint River. Flint residents knew the river water was not safe to drink because we had grown up hearing stories about General Motors dumping toxic waste into Flint River. But the voice of the community went unheeded, and Flint was appointed an emergency manager due to financial insolvency. This action removed the decision-making power and voice of the local government and community in an attempt to save money. Unfortunately, this type of action isn't uncommon in historically Black and Brown communities. Flint is a majority-Black and high-poverty city (54 percent and 41 percent respectively).

Untreated water coming from the polluted Flint River resulted in lead leaching from the water pipes. Many Flint residents became ill, several lost their lives, and today the children of Flint are still paying the price of growing up with lead poisoning from their water. What happened in Flint was a prime example of environmental racism. When a community has been racially stigmatized and objectified, it becomes easier for the privileged to silence that community's voice and make decisions for them that are not in their best interest. These are the effects of racism—the essential dehumanization of certain communities like Flint, and treating their residents as if they are disposable.

Flint is one of three majority-Black cities in Michigan that was taken over by state-appointed emergency managers who nullified or revoked the will of the residents in order to balance the books. Flint has joined a long list of predominantly Black and poor communities that are victims of environmental racism. Other examples include Asthma Alley in the South Bronx in New York (neighborhoods that are surrounded by highways and diesel-trucking companies);[9] Cancer Alley, an eighty-five-mile stretch in Louisiana from Baton Rouge to New Orleans, where there are more than 150 petrochemical plants along the Mississippi River;[10] and Port Arthur/Houston, Texas, which is home to the largest oil refinery in the U.S.[11] The issue of polluted land and contaminated water in nonwhite communities is nothing new.[12] How might we combat this manifestation of environmental elitism? As the people of God, we must not perpetuate the marginalization of the communities of color in our response to environmental negligence and abuse!

We all know that water is a necessity. It is vital to life. The need for clean, safe drinking water is a global issue. It is estimated that 3.575

9. Hazar Kilani, "'Asthma Alley': Why Minorities Bear Burden of Pollution Inequity Caused by White People," *The Guardian* (April 2019), https://www.theguardian.com/us-news/2019/apr/04/new-york-south-bronx-minorities-pollution-inequity.

10. Tristan Baurick, Lylla Younes, and Joan Meiners, "Welcome to 'Cancer Alley,' Where Toxic Air Is about to Get Worse," *ProPublica*, in partnership with *The Times-Picayune* and *The Advocate*, October 2019, https://www.propublica.org/article/welcome-to-cancer-alley-where-toxic-air-is-about-to-get-worse.

11. Ted Genoways, "Port Arthur, Texas: American Sacrifice Zone," Natural Resources Defense Council (November 2014), https://www.nrdc.org/onearth/port-arthur-texas-american-sacrifice-zone.

12. Christopher W. Tessum, Joshua S. Apte, Andrew L. Goodkind, Nicholas Z. Muller, Kimberley A. Mullins, David A. Paolella, Stephen Polasky, Nathaniel P. Springer, Sumil K. Thakrar, Julian D. Marshall, and Jason D. Hill, "Inequity in Consumption of Goods and Services Adds to Racial-Ethnic Disparities in Air Pollution Exposure," PNAS, March 2019 116 (13) 6006–6006, https://www.pnas.org/doi/full/10.1073/pnas.1818859116.

million people die from water-related diseases each year.[13] In fact, in the United States it caused 1.8 million deaths in 2015, according to a study published in *The Lancet*.[14] Every year, contaminated water sickens about a billion people.[15] Meanwhile, a third of the world does not even have access to safe drinking water![16] According to a report from the United Nations, "without safe drinking water, adequate sanitation, and hygiene facilities at home and in places of work and education, it is disproportionately harder for women and girls to lead safe, productive, healthy lives."[17]

There is a definitive water crisis in our world. Water is essential to life, yet "today 771 million people—1 in 10—lack access to safe water at home. The water crisis negatively impacts the health and livelihood of more than one-third of our global population."[18]

13. "Water Crisis Facts, Water.org, n.d., https://static.water.org/pdfs/Water%20Crisis%20 5-10.pdf.

14. "The Lancet: Pollution Linked to Nine Million Deaths Worldwide in 2015, Equivalent to 1 in 6 Deaths," Icahn School of Medicine at Mount Sinai (October 2017), https://www. mountsinai.org/about/newsroom/2017/the-lancet-pollution-linked-to-nine-million-deaths-worldwide-in-2015-equivalent-to-1-in-6-deaths.

15. "Water Pollution: Everything You Need to Know," Natural Resources Defense Council (April 2022), https://www.nrdc.org/stories/water-pollution-everything-you-need-know#:~:-text=On%20human%20health&text=Contaminated%20water%20can%20also%20make,-to%20the%20most%20polluting%20industries

16. "1 in 3 People Globally Do Not Have Access to Safe Drinking Water—UNICEF, WHO," World Health Organization (June 2019), https://www.who.int/news/item/18-06-2019-1-in-3-people-globally-do-not-have-access-to-safe-drinking-water-unicef-who.

17. "Water and Gender," United Nations, n.d., https://www.unwater.org/water-facts/water-and-gender.

18. "About Us," Water.org, https://water.org/about-us/.

This unit is titled "I Am We," which conveys the South African philosophy of *ubuntu*. *Ubuntu* is a word that is rich with meaning. It originates from the Zulu people of South Africa (Zulu pronunciation: [ùɓúntʼù]). *Ubuntu* means "humanity," but it recognizes the humanity of all as created in the image of God, thus making the image of God the essence of humanity's identity. As Suzanne Membe-Metale affirms, *ubuntu* is a spirituality that enables mutual sharing and satisfaction. It can be illustrated in the biblical account of the disciples sharing all they had with one another so that no one lacked anything (see Acts 4:32–35). *Ubuntu* is sometimes translated, "I am because we are," or, "I am because you are." *Ubuntu* is essentially about togetherness and how all of our actions have an impact on others and on society. *Ubuntu* is a helpful concept for understanding the manifestation of the image of God and how interconnected God's good creation is, as well as humanity's relationship with itself.

There was a white anthropologist who had been studying the habits and culture of a remote African tribe. He had been working in the village for quite some time, and the day before he was to return home, he put together a gift basket filled with delicious fruits from around the region and wrapped it in a ribbon. He placed the basket under a tree and gathered up the children in the village.

The man drew a line in the dirt, looked at the children, and said, "When I tell you to start, run to the tree. Whoever gets there first will win the basket of fruit."

When he told them to run, they all joined hands and ran together to the tree. Then they sat around the basket and enjoyed their treat as a group.

The anthropologist was shocked. He asked why they would all go together when one of them could have won all the fruit for themselves.

A young girl looked up at him and said, "How can one of us be happy if all the other ones are sad?"

She was saying, *I am we!*

REFLECT AND DISCUSS

- Thinking about Cain's response to God when God asked about Abel, how do you react when someone suggests you have done something offensive? Do you accept responsibility and move to make amends, or is your first instinct, like Cain, to deny, blame, or placate?

- How do you define "sin"? Before answering this, consider how sin impacts you and your relationship to God, your relationship to yourself, your relationship to others, and your relationship to earth.

- As you think about the implications of Genesis 4, whom would you define as "your neighbor?" Do they have to live close by? Are they all human?

- What are some of the connections you're making on how caring for creation also works against racism?

- How have you noticed disparities in who is most affected by environmental oppression and exploitation and those who are affected the least?

- Commodification is the transformation of goods and services into commodities. How have you witnessed the commodification of water disproportionately impact people of color where you live or in other places around the world? What can you do about it?

- If you are in a place of privilege, what role do you play in environmental protest movements in communities of color?

If you have come here to help me you are wasting your time,
but if you have come because your liberation is bound up
with mine, then let us work together.
—Attributed to Lilla Watson

RESPOND

Grow Outward

Discover what the local environmental issues are where you live and take action. History reveals to us that even a small group of people can have an immense impact when we decide to show up together!

- Connect with your local chapter of Interfaith Power & Light. Check out interfaithpowerandlight.org to find further resources.

- Visit the Evangelical Environmental Network at creationcare.org and click "Take Action" on the "Get Involved" tab to get ideas.

- Connect with your local city council representative and get involved in what is happening around you!

Grow Inward

There are many organizations working toward water justice today. Take an hour this week and dive into some research for your zip code or state. What are the water issues near you? Who is already working on the problems, and how can you join them?

Make an active effort to listen to the people of color in your community and ask how you can join them in the struggle and walk alongside them. Learn how people in your area may be oppressed by unjust environmental policies. How might your congregation stand with those whose voices are ignored or silenced?

Form a Green Habit

One practical way to fight against the privatization of water is by buying reusable water bottles. If you spent $1.09 on one plastic water bottle, you could refill that bottle every day for the next eight years before spending a dollar's worth of tap water! The issue of privatization also intersects the issue of plastic waste, which is another huge problem for the planet today, especially in our water systems.

ABOUT THE AUTHORS

CALEB CRAY HAYNES is cofounder of Nazarenes for Creation Care. He is an ordained elder in the Church of the Nazarene and the community creation pastor at Kaleo Nashville. Caleb is the author of *Garbage Theology: The Unseen World of Waste and What It Means for the Salvation of Every Person, Every Place, and Every Thing,* and frequently speaks on issues of faith and the environment. He is a partner with the Evangelical Environmental Network. Caleb holds a BA in religion and philosophy from Trevecca Nazarene University and is studying theology and ecology at Nazarene Theological College in Manchester, UK. Caleb lives in Nashville, Tennessee, with his wife and two daughters. Connect at calebcrayhaynes.com.

RYAN FASANI is a pastor, writer, and farmer, which is to say he tries to point people toward the holy, sees things and jots them down, and believes Wendell Berry is a saint. He's a sought-after speaker and storyteller but is in highest demand for his organic lettuce. He's an ordained elder in the Church of the Nazarene and a church planter who is currently starting a church-planting and ministry incubator in Washington State. He lives on a farm with his wife, four kids, and seven milk goats. Connect with Fasani's other writing—his memoir, *Consuming Hope,* and his two books on rethinking the Christian faith, *Walking Trees* and *Curated Coals*—at his website, ryanfasani.com.

MEGAN M. PARDUE has been the lead pastor at Refuge Home Church in Durham, North Carolina, since 2013. She is an ordained elder in the Church of the Nazarene and a graduate of Southern Nazarene University and Duke Divinity School. In addition to pastoring, she teaches preaching at Duke Divinity School and co-hosts the weekly lectionary preaching podcast, A Plain Account. Megan enjoys growing a large vegetable and flower garden and raising chickens on her lot in the city. She lives in Durham with her husband, Keith, and their two children.

TODD WOMACK is a social worker currently serving as a lecturer and academic advisor at the University of Michigan–Flint in the social work department. He is an ordained elder in the Church of the Nazarene and co-pastors The Underground Church, which is a church for netizens that speaks boldly to the issues of injustice in the world framed in the orientation of peace-building work. His passion for racial equity and equality is evident in his continued dedication and work toward strengthening Flint neighborhoods and supporting realistic and solution-focused experiences. He and his wife, Roshanda, are the proud parents of three boys: Ngozi ("blessing"), Osei ("noble"), and Ande ("unwavering").

We would like to express huge thanks to our editors Brenda and Laurie Braaten.

www.ingramcontent.com/pod-product-compliance
Lightning Source LLC
Chambersburg PA
CBHW081551040426
42448CB00016B/3286